City of Departures

HELEN TOOKEY was born near Leicester in 1969. She is now based in Liverpool, where she teaches creative writing at Liverpool John Moores University. She studied philosophy and English literature at university, and has published critical work about writers including Anaïs Nin and Malcolm Lowry. Her debut collection *Missel-Child* (Carcanet, 2014) was shortlisted for the Seamus Heaney Centre Prize for First Full Collection. Her pamphlet *In the Glasshouse* was published by HappenStance Press in 2016, and the CD/booklet *If You Put Out Your Hand*, a collaboration with musician Sharron Kraus, came out from Wounded Wolf Press in 2016. She has recently been collaborating with composer and sound artist Martin Heslop, putting text together with electronic soundscapes.

Also by Helen Tookey

Missel-Child (Carcanet 2014)

HELEN TOOKEY

City of Departures

CARCANET

First published in Great Britain in 2019 by
Carcanet Press Ltd
Alliance House, 30 Cross Street
Manchester M2 7AQ
www.carcanet.co.uk

A CfP catalogue record for this book is available from the British Library

ISBN 978 1 78410 759 8

The publisher acknowledges financial assistance from Arts Council England

Typeset in England by XL Publishing Services, Exmouth
Printed and bound in England by SRP Ltd, Exeter

Contents

I

Equinox	9
City of Departures	10
Painting the Sitting-Room Door	11
Hors-la-loi	12
Stone Garden	13
On the Black Canal	14
Chapel	15
Boat	16
Halb null	17

II

Being Mary Lennox	21
Prairie	22
Leonora	23
In the Rose Garden	24
At the Ponds	25
Classroom	26
Signal	27
Green	28
Aviary	29
Rhododendron Garden	30
Front	32
Blueprint	33

III

Hotel Apostrophe	37
Only Windows	39
Chinese White	40
Funeral Procession of Mourners and Musicians, Ming Dynasty, about 1400	42
Aftermaths	43
Letter to Anna	46

What Can We Still Do   47
Strandgade (Ida Hammershøi)   49

IV

Map   53
Speicherstadt   54
Scenes from a Bright Town   55
Observance   57
Paper Birds   58
Under the Hill   59
St James' Gardens   60
Louise   61
Quend-Plage-les-Pins   62
Mow Cop   63

Skizzen / Sketches   67

Notes   79
Acknowledgements   82

I

Equinox

The year is balanced, for a moment only.
Disequilibrium is the rule: of course,

we know that. We can't find a ritual,
stare at our hands, which are stubbornly blank.

In my dream the twins were fighting,
each hell-bent on her own direction.

Conjoined at the shoulder: muscles pulling,
bones grinding under the skin –

a bird, an angel, at violent odds
with its own winged nature. You text me

to tell me you've broken a cup,
burned the toast, melted the handle

on the stovetop coffee-pot. We say *equinox*
as though the word were a stay against chaos,

a blocking spell against all the unmakings
massing like static, heading our way.

City of Departures

When I stepped out of the house the air held rain, the scent of it, the taste. The light was bruised and yellowish. A blackbird was singing, very clearly, his song amplified by the coming rain. The scene felt familiar, already lived-through. The caption was *Morning in the city of departures.* I was walking through narrow streets close to the docks, under the piers of bridges, through brick archways. The cobblestones were wet and I had on no shoes. There had been a railway accident, journeys were disrupted or rendered impossible. You didn't appear and yet you were present, if only in the feeling of missed connections. You were there in the sense of having spoken a vital word to me and then gone away, leaving me wandering the wet quaysides holding the word I couldn't use, a bright coin in the wrong currency.

Painting the Sitting-Room Door

She said she didn't know why.

Perhaps it was the new month, the hinge of it
swinging open, bringing the first
sharp frost of the year.

Perhaps it was the wolf-moon, its hard
rising, its boneyard stare
at her kitchen window.

Or perhaps it was her dream of skating
out over the frozen pond, trusting the ice
as a bird trusts the air.

She said the door had been white already
but now gleamed in its whiteness, seemed taller,
seemed insistently more itself

and her small room, with its books
and plants, its colourful rugs, now a door
to a snow-field, a cold clear plain of thought

that called to her with a high tune, a thin song
like the winter taste of biting on metal.

Hors-la-loi

he is forty-six years old
and his hands are a sculptor's hands

in the daytime we lie on warm stone
we drink sunlight through our skin

he reads me with his palms
his fingers are cruxes

root-patterns   river-branchings

my father is a jackdaw
squabbling with himself out in the yard

at night we slip through the canvas
the forest becomes us

my father cannot follow
slow-witted   slow-footed

clumsy hunter   we laugh at him

and he shatters like moonlight
over the dead leaves

Stone Garden

Stone trees grow here. Yellow eyes
peer down: lit windows,

clockface gods. The river-road
is back-projected. Headlights trail

plasma fingers, blue-white flux
beyond the palings. We read sound

through our spines – the quarter-chimes
that draw in air the outline

of this hour, open the borders
and close them again.

Stone pulls: we lose definition, sink
to the forest-floor. Something in us

is giving, as the repurposed city
breaks and gives, black water pushing

at the dock-gates, lapping
at the stone steps, ships

coming in and in on the flood-tide.

On the Black Canal

Your boat is moored on the black canal
and the woman is playing the cello for you,

low notes the colour of crows' wings.
You are a sound-box, air vibrates inside your bones

as each note elongates, a dark expanse –
are you under her protection, or is it a baffle

she draws around you, words becoming lost
in the rasp of bow against wire, your skull

full of overtones. Where were you trying to go that day
you crossed the fields when the planes came,

droning low, forcing you down with the weight
of sound – you lay it seemed for hours,

pressed to the earth, unable to move
till the sound cleared, the weight eased

from your bones and you ran, away from
the terror of air, the fields' aphasic spaces.

Where were you going? You can't remember, and now
you're moored in the long box of your boat, and the woman

is playing the cello for you, the sound closing
over your head like black water, like crows' wings.

Chapel

But it wasn't like this, she says.
Not when I saw it before.

She can't say when she saw it before.
Only, she knows she has carried it since.

There were candles, she says. A plain wooden cross.
There were dry leaves whispering in corners,

ivy, and elder, and bitter apples.
A difficult harvest, she says,

but exact. Something was here,
she says. Something remained.

Boat

So did you maybe dream it – that wrecked boat
uncovered by storm, by shifted sand,
for just one day? A year and more

you'd walked that beach in all weathers
and there'd never been a boat: only that day,
the day she left you, and you walked the beach

as always, because what else could you do
– only that day was there a boat, bleached and broken,
a thing of ribs, with just enough hull

to make a holding; so you crept inside, curled up
and lay for hours, until the sheer indifference
of wind and sea brought some kind of peace

and next day again there was no boat
and when you asked you were told
there had never been a boat; and maybe not dream

but surely deep need had fetched it, if only
for those few hours, back into its being
as a thing that holds, that keeps afloat –

Halb null

It occurred to me to ask the time. She said *Halb null*. Half an hour to zero. How did it get so late? We had done nothing, only dallied in the café in the square, eating bread and artichokes, using up time to no purpose, and yet with a long journey to make. Halb null, and we had not even set out!

There were road blocks, long queues of traffic out of the city. At a standstill alongside a wide flat field, we watched circus performers rehearsing, tossing fire-sticks to each other in complicated patterns and interweavings. Sometimes they missed their catches, laughed as the fire-sticks fell harmlessly at their feet. It was late and they were only rehearsing, there was no sense of urgency or concern among them. But for us, time had slipped through our fingers, it seemed that we might never get back.

II

Being Mary Lennox

Everything is yellow, because of the heat.
You are thin and sour, like spoiled milk,
like bad-wishing. A yellow girl. A thin little thing.

Everything happens at a distance: first the parties,
then the deaths. *Cholera*, that is hands gripping,
tightening round throats. *Veranda*, that is the sound

of a miniature teaspoon tapping tapping
at a bone china cup. In the house, one room
becomes another, a string of rooms

like paper dolls. The dining room's best –
the tiny plates, the pretty silver knives. You nibble
at a biscuit, taste the strong sweetish wine.

With a stiff little bow you announce to no one:
I am Mary Lennox. Then with the flat of your hand
you send the whole scene flying.

Prairie

Sometimes we are girls, and sometimes horses.

When we're horses, we can gallop, but there aren't so many stories.

When we're girls, we wear calico dresses and never any shoes.

Calico is always striped, like sticks of rock, and crackles when we run.

Sometimes we live in the dug-out, and sometimes in the new house.

The new house is made of shiny yellow wood, and has real glass windows that really open.

The new house is square, like a doll's house, and sits exactly flat on the ground.

The new house smells of yellow wood, and all the rooms are clean and empty, bright boxes of yellow air.

There are no other houses anywhere, only prairie.

The dug-out is dark and cool and makes us feel like hunters.

The dug-out smells of earth and is full of the sound of water, the creek running just below.

We lie flat on our bellies and watch the water-creatures, and we are something like the water-creatures, or like otters perhaps, thin and brown and sharp-eyed, slipping silently into the water, speaking the urgent language of hunters.

This is the unrolling of *prairie*.

Prairie is the widest word we know.

Leonora

At first you're a child, out of scale
with the house you find yourself inside

but you inhabit the space like a spider, you clamber
and climb and spin rope-ladders.

You put salt in the sugar, your mother and father
grind their teeth, but it gets them nowhere.

You spend hours in the greenhouse, rewriting the labels
on the little glass bottles, from *Poison* to *Drink Me*.

You were the smallest, but now you've grown bigger
so you pick them up between thumb and forefinger

– mother, father, brother, brother –
and fix them all in the painting, whistling

as you hang them crooked over the fireplace
then let in the animals, let yourself out

through the trapdoor you've made
in the dining-room table.

In the Rose Garden

She's in the rose garden again, staring
at her right arm, its pale soft underside
that never gets the sun, never gets tanned.

It's very strange, she thinks, because the veins
at her wrist are greenish-blue: but the blood
that's blossoming, overblown already,

dropping fat petals on her dress, her shoes,
the path with its edging of sharp pointed
tiles (*weathered* is the word she'll later hear

and not understand) – the blood is brilliant
startling red, much redder than the clouds
of dark pink roses tangled above her –

red, and at its heart a splinter, a glimpse
of white, bright as the spiny shells that mark
the drop from the patio, where her parents

and the others are talking, moving their
mouths and making gestures, though the sound
doesn't reach her – the drop from the patio

down to the lawn, and all the way beyond
to where she is, in the rose garden, staring
at her right arm, its strange new blossoming.

At the Ponds

She brings you to the ponds, where the people are lying under the water. They are women, children, men – whole families.

Looking up through the water and the starry weeds, they must see a green world. A floating arch, studded with brilliant stars that waver in their green sky.

When it starts to rain, as it does now, it must be warm and soft under the water, the sky forming and re-forming in small expanding circles.

The people look so peaceful, even the children! Every now and then a hand moves, or a foot, just a small slow shift so that the water-plants wave gently and sometimes glitter where they break the surface, and then settle back again to stillness.

Well?, she says, and you remember, back at the castle, on the wooden bridge, how you would pause and half look down and catch just a glimpse of the thick white stems of the lilies they said would catch at you and drag you down if you ever went into the water – just a glimpse and then you would look quickly away before you could see them, the souls who must be there, caught and kept fast among the lilies, women, children, men, lying in the green water and gazing unblinkingly up at you as you stood on the warm smooth planks of the bridge –

Classroom

there is never any sound

there is only light   the drifts of it
glittering columns   slow as church

she has asked him already
now they both turn to look at me

her mouth moves   shaping a question
I can't answer

the moment expands
the three of us   caught in its hang

falling through it
like chalk dust through sunlight

Signal

Those nights when you woke and knew at once
something was different. Not the steady sound
of your brother's breath, as he steered through sleep
in the bunk above – not a sound at all
but something that tugged, drew you from dream
to pull back the curtains

and there riding the black sky
the moon's bright diode, transmitting
it seemed straight to you, but the signal scrambled
by the flickering leaves of the chestnut tree,
reaching you as unreadable scatter, pulses of light
falling into the dark of the room, a code
you never learned to decipher.

Green

You slip through the gap in the sandstone wall
and turn in among the trees,
the stone-grey columns of beech.

The sound of your steps is hollow, the path
dry and cracked after so little rain.
Bramble and nettle and falls of ivy

half screen the space of the field,
where a few people are walking their dogs,
small children are chasing a ball.

You are, or might be, a boy in a hide
keeping watch through the long afternoons,
held tight as a closed fist

inside the pleasure of not being seen
– but after a while the feeling comes
that something does see you,

some thin persistent tendril
involving itself in you, like the bindweed
that twines itself along the hedgerows

and with a quick convulsive shake of the mind
you get going, telling yourself
it's time anyway you were heading back.

Aviary

The sound of rain falling on the gardens makes me think of my uncle. My uncle kept birds in an aviary. I never knew what kind they were, only that they were small and pretty, little yellow birds that fluttered and perched on the specially arranged branches behind the wire mesh. My uncle was a quiet man and he liked to be out of the noise and busyness of the house, down at the end of the garden tending to his birds. I suppose they must have been different birds at different times, such little birds couldn't have lived for many years, but I never thought of that when I was a child, only that my uncle kept birds in an aviary.

I liked the word *aviary*. It felt light and airy, it seemed to flutter like a dance, like lace curtains shifting in a breeze. It seemed to hold something of girls' names, Ava, Evie, the pretty sort of name I had always wanted but didn't have. As though an aviary might be a room full of girls in white and yellow muslin dresses, fluttering in the breeze.

After my uncle died, my aunt tried to look after the birds. But it had always been my uncle who looked after them, I don't think she really knew what had to be done. So my cousin arranged for the birds to be taken away. I don't know where they were taken. I suppose to another aviary, since they wouldn't have known how to fend for themselves. But it would be nice to think of my cousin and my aunt simply opening the wire mesh and setting the birds free. As though in that room full of girls someone had flung open the windows, and all the girls had gathered their skirts and scrambled up onto the sills, ready to fly –

Rhododendron Garden

The path to the Rhododendron Garden is one kilometre long.

Frequent curves, and after every curve, another length of path. Transverse to the path, cutting down the slope, run-off channels. Black ditches overhung with ferns. Water taking the quickest way.

To help you find your way to the Rhododendron Garden, and to let you know how far you have walked, we have placed eight equidistant numbered marker posts along the route.

You don't see any marker posts after no. 3.
You begin to be a little afraid of it, this path.

How green the light is, how dense, because of the trees. The height of them. Sometimes, the enormous deaths of them. Their deaths persist, they inhabit their deaths, continuing to stand, to occupy their own outlines, only – you suppose – becoming very slowly less solid, hollowing out from the inside –

The last marker (number 8) is on the southern edge of the Rhododendron Garden.

The rhododendron-trees are smooth, slim, reddish-brown. The branches seem to grow straight from the earth, at first separate, then entwined. Thickness of leaves underfoot. Winding paths, little bridges. A pleasure garden, laid out and forgotten. *This part of the garden was abandoned and overgrown during the War –*

Moss at your feet, tiny green stars, seafloor eyes. Little bridges. *This beautiful place* – Like somebody tracing circles with their finger on your palm. *Round and round the garden.* But they don't finish the trick, they leave the rhyme hanging –

Little bridges. The chain of sunken gardens on the sea-front, with their streams, their flights of miniature steps. But they were in the sunshine, and in the evenings there were strings of coloured lights. No, not those bright gardens – look again –

This time you see the two girls standing on the small arched bridge: the Japanese-style garden, the girls laughing, sharing a secret. You are in the trees, not hiding exactly, or at least you didn't set out to hide, but now you find you're not willing to be seen, knowing quite well that if you allow the two girls to realise your presence they will instantly close up, their faces shut and unsmiling, their laughter flicking off as though someone had tripped a switch –

Front

When we reached the sea-front I was at a loss. The front as I had known it – the busy road with its hotels and coloured lights, the children's boating lake with its blue and yellow paddle-boats – was no longer there. Only a drab road running parallel to low scrubby dunes, with the occasional trampled path leading off through them, and beyond the dunes, the flat sand, and the sea.

A couple who were walking nearby stopped and looked at me curiously, their attention caught by my puzzlement, which began to give way to distress as I tried to explain what I had been expecting to see. – But it hasn't been like that for a very long time, they said. Not since *before* –

And I understood what they meant. It was impossible that I should have seen it that way. But I knew I had.

Blueprint

When he saw the design my young companion laughed. *How are we going to make this?* The blueprint looked so complicated – it seemed to call for springs and levers and pieces of equipment that perhaps didn't even exist, certainly that we had no access to. And not only that, what was the design in the end supposed to achieve? And where should we begin?

We spread out the design on the floor of our small circular room and stepped carefully around it, looking at it from all angles. I wanted to see what he would suggest. He was a member of nothing in the world and that, I felt sure, gave him a particular insight. We didn't even have a language in common, yet I trusted that we would find a way to communicate. I believed that he could speak and understand many languages, such as the languages of the birds and the languages of the trees, which were mostly closed to me. He knelt on the floor, the afternoon light catching his strangely happy face. I couldn't tell whether we were prisoners in our tower room or had the freedom of the whole world.

III

Hotel Apostrophe

Apostrophe. 1. Rhet. *A figure of speech, by which a speaker or writer*
suddenly stops in his discourse, and turns to address pointedly
some person or thing, either present or absent; an exclamatory address.

As though the ordinary business of *being a hotel* were the discourse,
which has suddenly been abandoned, the notional *hotel* turning
instead to address us.

Everything points to it, from the moment we step through the
opening in the wall marked *Accès piéton.* The huge tree with three
branches of equal thickness, as though suggesting three different
ways, but there is only the one way, down concrete steps through
the broken passageway. High on the concrete wall, some kind of
flywheel, no longer connected to anything. The overgrown courtyard,
loggia thick with ivy, blank spaces of missing windows. All of this, a
preliminary address –

some person or thing, either present or absent –

We are not the absent ones. Certainly, though, there is an absence.
Everything remarks upon it, indeed *insists* upon it. On the veranda,
rows of armchairs and occasional tables, carefully provided with
coasters and ashtrays for drinks and cigarettes. In the downstairs
hall, the display cabinet, mahogany, glass-fronted, lined with yellow
satin, displaying nothing. On the landing, the mirror, gilt-framed,
propped on the rosewood sewing-machine table (maker's name,
Opel, elegantly incorporated into the wrought iron framework
supporting the table, that is, Adam Opel of Rüsselsheim, engineer
first of sewing-machines, having witnessed with his own eyes this
new technology in Paris in 1858 and been possessed of both the
visionary imagination and the engineering acumen to realise its
potential, latterly persuaded by his five sons into the more modern
business of the design and manufacture of bicycles, and Adam Opel
AG eventually – but Adam himself long dead by this point – coming
to be known for the design and manufacture of automobiles) – the

mirror carefully angled to reflect only the blank yellowish space of the opposite wall

– and returning to the veranda with its rows of empty armchairs, this time we notice the metalwork objects placed in the window-niches, suggesting something of creatures, something of clocks, but not exactly either: some kind of serious toys, as though of a watchmaker who doesn't want to tell the hours, an astronomer who doesn't want to see the stars –

Only Windows

suppose the house were only windows
or outlines of windows   panels of air
that pivot slowly through their angles

the house therefore a kind of drift
we can never quite catch   can't get a fix on
our words for rooms no longer of use

harboured unharboured   a frequent reversal
a summer dress   pulled through itself
turned wrong side out   let fall to the floor

Chinese White

December 4, 1843

Gentlemen,

You have wished me to record my opinion of the pigment which you call Chinese White and I do so without hesitation.

Since you introduced it now some years ago I have unhesitatingly used it, having in the first instance obtained the opinion of one of our most distinguished chemists as regards its durability. This being favourable in the most satisfactory degree, all my scruples were removed, and ever since, my own practical experience has led me to confide in it, so that I no longer have the least doubt – none of my pictures give the least evidence of any change.

I am Gentlemen your obedient servant...

It made the family name.

Tested by Faraday, approved by Ruskin,
they say it caused chaos in Rathbone Place, the street jammed
with the carriages of all the best painters in London, clamouring
for this new white that didn't dull, didn't fade

and William and Henry making sure
to get it in writing.

Now (grandfather Henry long dead, Rathbone Place
flattened by bombs, colours mixed in the new factory
fifteen miles out west at Harrow) it's the white fronts
of these Regency streets that draw our gaze –

the thin lines of these window-frames,
these sills and sashes, and the long dress
of the woman who waits on the bright pavement
for her cue to move, which never comes.

It's the clear glaze that removes all trace
of your painting hand, that leaves your skies
the perfect blue of jasperware, only
the clouds' undersides tinged with yellow

and the faces of your buildings so unbroken
we want to touch them, to find a way in.

Funeral Procession of Mourners and Musicians, Ming Dynasty, about 1400

All the objects in this case were once buried in the tombs of the wealthy

twenty-four figures on foot
and four on horseback

hands and arms poised to make music
but their instruments missing

they are mime artists now   each making
a different gesture – precise cuppings
& shapings of air

they are a procession   and even here
in this bright glass case   each remembers
his place exactly

even the horses

short-legged and sturdy   each still
with his shiny saddle   each
with his carefully coloured mane

(one white   one green
two dark yellow)

they too remember their role
and are patient

though surely also puzzled

by this persistent gleaming light
this long lacking of the dead

Aftermaths

Newton's London pictures are beautiful but also terrible... They are
not topographical views but aftermaths...
Andrew Graham-Dixon, *The Peculiarity of*
Algernon Newton (Daniel Katz Gallery, 2012)

They said *a toy London,*
quaint, but of cardboard.

They said *tranquillity.*

Did they not see the shadow – how it pooled
across the streets, how it deepened?

*

Canals have always seen too much.
The blinded windows, the black
thin trees – they swallow everything
whole, show you precisely
what they have taken.
They will never give it back.

*

Even in the morning, the trees lean
like broken men.

*

43

It is a case of rising
and shining – of ironing out
the quirks. One window
repeats another. There must be
no question of distinguishing,
of stepping out of line.

★

For once, a tiny man, a tiny woman.
Perhaps they have come out
from their black front door
to walk a little way along the pavement?
But the plane tree in the courtyard-garden
is many times taller than they
and if they are to turn the corner
they must reckon with the black cloak
it will throw across them.

★

As the blue comes on, the canal
shivers, and just for a second
all the charts go haywire.
(Reflection of telegraph pole,
of factory chimney.)
In the ward of the white house
no one will sleep. The single lamp outside
will burn all night.

★

You could turn, walk back
the way you came – the open fields
with their sudden patches of black.

But, of course, you can't.
There is only the going-forward,
and the gap.

Letter to Anna

Dear Anna, I shall come to you in November, all being well. They are making plans to close the borders, but I believe there is a little time yet.

Dear Anna, I am thinking of you in your city of water. Do you remember, when we walked out along the rampart, we saw so many herons, sitting silent in the trees like huge grey sentinels, we were almost scared, though we laughed about it afterwards.

Dear Anna, it is still summer here, but so heavy, it drags on one, it weighs one down. Yesterday I walked to the field to pick blackberries (they are early this year), and I got a good bowlful, but even such a short walk made me so tired. I think it must be fresher where you are.

Dear Anna, I look often at your picture, though I could wish he had not made it quite so sad – that look in your eyes, so far away, and that tilt of your head, as though you are listening for something, but you do not really believe it will come. There is something in the hands, too – somehow I think he has made them too large, almost like a man's hands, they seem to lie in your lap so awkwardly, as though you had yet to grow into them, yet to discover what they could be for.

Dear Anna, I have applied for my papers and shall come to you in November. I do not know whether there will be another opportunity. Please expect me.

What Can We Still Do

Do you remember our first telephone conversations?
Do you remember how you always despaired a little?
Perhaps you could try to send me an invitation?

How far away or how close are you?
Would you still accept it now?
Try it, write to me, ask me!

What does that mean anyway – 'somewhere in Paris'?
And would you want to see me?
Let me know if receiving more letters might help!

Do you think you would be able to come to Austria this winter?
Or would you rather come to Paris?
Perhaps we should meet in Zürich?

Tell me how you feel about it!
And also tell me what you are doing and thinking!
And do not worry too much!

Can I expect you? Or can I not?
In any case, why America?
Do you know what I mean by that?

Will you send me the translations?
Could you write to me at the Kirchgasse address?
If only we could see each other!

Did the little calendar and the two notebooks arrive?
Say something about the events in the train to Frankfurt.
Be good to me!

Can you really not write to me?
You should, you must write to me.
Will you understand me nonetheless?

Could we not join hands here and exchange a few words?
Could I come soon and help you find a lamp?
What can we still do? Tell me.

Strandgade (Ida Hammershøi)

other men made statues
begged them to become women

he wants me as a statue
or no   not a statue   not the likeness of a real woman

I am a column   a pillar of black   the only relief my pale neck
beneath roundish mass of pinned-up hair

a pillar of salt   that was Lot's wife
punished because she turned her head
turned to look back at the city in flames

a pillar of salt   that might have been beautiful
glittering white in that place of heat
sparkling like stars against the blue of the sky

here we live as though under water
long afternoons lap at our windows
feel their way over ceilings and floors

I am blurred to the colour of a thought that won't form
a memory   wish   that won't come clear

my head is bowed, but to no work
I sit at the piano, but do not play

I stare into angles, arrangements of objects
    that make no sense
I stand holding a broom, but do not sweep

and doors   always doors

their rectangles repeat in my mind
their handles baffle me   what are they for

it has become a habit   not knowing
not remembering   how to proceed

I am a vessel   slowly filling with water

I think one day he will set down his brush
he will bid me turn around
and there will be no one to comprehend

IV

Map

I watch her from the station, all the way
down the long straight street to the museum of modern art.
How she walks, very neat, in the space of herself,
her black hair and boxy coat
marking the boundaries, the solid shape
of her against not-her.

I see her later in the garden,
down on the lawn, her back to me,
looking out across the blue cold water.
I know she's been drawn down the shallow steps
carved in the earth-bank, between the trees'
intricate roots. I know she hoped
she could get to the beach, stand on the narrow
stony strip and choose a pebble,
drop it deep in the keep of her pocket.

I want to ask her to draw me a map
of how she came here, of every decision
that led to this place, this afternoon.
I want to ask her to lay her map
down over mine, watch me turn them
till they find their alignment, coming to meet
at this single point, then heading away.

Speicherstadt

You and I in the Speicherstadt,
in the basement with the picture-restorers.
You examine the brickwork
while Bernd takes photos, measuring the damage.
– These places are built to flood, he says,
but they shouldn't have put this flooring in.
See how it buckles? Because the water can't get out.

Later, at the Elphi, we take a ticket
to enter the gleaming white tunnel, to ride
the silver moving-staircase that carries us up
through eight floors of warehouse
to the triumph of the Plaza, all glow
and reflection, all of us caught and multiplied
in the curved glass walls, the openings
to shops and bars – the way out
to the observation deck
deliberately a little harder to find
and the air so cold it numbs our hands

but we stand looking out at the river's grey reach
and the wide grey expanse of sky
just a thin line of pinkish light breaking the cloud
away to the south, beyond the yards
where a navy supply ship lies under repair,
hunkered down, not ready to leave.

Scenes from a Bright Town

... a bright, clean-looking town...
Ward Lock Guide to Wales, 1966

Eight a.m.

the long beach is almost empty
and the sea is quiet, its attention elsewhere

like a small girl in Sunday school
who sits on a hard chair, half-attending

pleating and unpleating
the hem of her skirt

Sycamore

and at the upstairs window the sycamore tree
rustling its bunches of yellow keys
as though to say *there are doors not tried*
as though to say *there are other ways*

Garden

not midnight exactly – three minutes past
by the kitchen clock
but the garden is sudden and strange in the moonlight:
thorn trees, battlements, everything a knife-edge
version of itself, sky a scumble
of silver clouds, and the garden become
a gleaming box, a Schauspielhaus

Castle Sands

but this beach is made from fragments of shell
thinnest flakings of mother-of-pearl

as though a child had run with a stick
through a city built of fine bone china

had run and run and kept on running
till he ran himself clean out of story
and we now in some far future
sift the pieces through our fingers

try to reconstruct the city

Observance

At nine she comes to unlock the garden.
June at its deepest: drift of seedheads, air
dense with messages. Winter is not
to be imagined – how could we lie again
unheld in the long dark?

As she turns at the foot of the stone steps
her right hand brushes the lavender's
pale spikes, a quick pinch releasing
the scent to her fingers – gesture seeming
unconsidered, as she might without knowing
smooth back her hair

yet an observance. She carries the day
back to the house, the curtained rooms.

Paper Birds

This girl, who chooses not to speak,
has perhaps made a study of trees –
how perfectly they express in every part

their meaning, which is simply *tree*;
how they are never in error, nor misunderstood.
Maybe it's the gap she's afraid of, the split that opens

every time between the thought, the wish,
and what is said; and she's observed, maybe,
how once the thing is said it stays for all time

said, accreting wrongness of all kinds
and from all sides, the way that shiny things
(the mantelpiece, the mirror on the chest of drawers)

attract the dust. I admire her steadfastness,
her singleness of mind, as she sits, smiling
or shaking her head in response to questions,

making in silence her intricate paper birds.

Under the Hill

I saw you in the morning   circling the hill
your cry   grieving a loss
ash on the wind   which of us

ddu   the darkness
tongue against teeth
ddu   ddu
breath against bone

I met you in the earth-hold   place of gifts
whisper of wind   through dry leaves
through cockle-shells   which of us

ddu   the darkness
tongue against teeth
ddu   ddu
breath against bone

under the hill   you buried me
now   you recover me
sound-box   ruined body

you need me hollow
how else should I sing

St James' Gardens

there is water lying on the flagstones

a phrase repeats   *departed this life*

as though   happening to glance up
at the mantelpiece clock   and understanding

the time was come   they stood
and quietly gathered their things

and murmuring without reproach
an appropriate word   left the room

turning only to pull the door
very gently   quite securely   closed

Louise

Tonight you have set out all the keys on the oak table. They lie on the grained and pitted surface, each with its own design, finials of love-knots, triquetras, plain oval loops. You align them carefully, crosswise to the grain, you lay them out as you would lay out the cards for a reading, and you wait for a long time. But you find nothing to unlock.

It is no longer autumn, so yesterday you burned the few dried leaves from the mantelpiece. Some blackened instantly, shrank into themselves, became scraps of ash and then became nothing. But others unfolded in the flames, their ribs and veins glowing like wires, and one, a fireleaf, gleamed like a phoenix and flew, rising out of sight and up towards the black night sky.

Where is Louise? The pictures on the walls, they are not Louise, and the body in the long mirror, that is not Louise's body. You remember the time you saw her stand in the gap, the split in the beech's hollow trunk, and you remember your fear, that the tree would close over. You called to her to come away, and she laughed, of course, she was never afraid –

– No. She is somewhere under a clear cold sky, in a country of endless unchanging light. She is pulling a sledge across miles of snow, skirting the pinewoods. There is no sound, only the steady crunch of her boots on the hard-packed snow, and the rasp of the sledge's metal runners, this sledge she pulls like a kind of companion. She doesn't speak, but as you watch her you come to see that there is a kind of speaking here, a syntax of endless unfolding, of no end-point and no desire, only this walking over snow, this pulling a sledge forever in half-light.

Quend-Plage-les-Pins

This place would be beautiful
if it didn't exist. Well – the pines
can stay, and the dunes, with their strange
tenacious grasses; and the fine
falling sand, and the waves,
long and slanted, coming in
and coming in.
          But it wouldn't need
this road, with its ribbons
and pennants, its kites and crêpes
and beach-toys. It wouldn't need
this fairground, this car-park,
this promenade. It wouldn't need
a name. It wouldn't need us.

Mow Cop

Today is a new month and Hiroshige
has painted *The City Flourishing*. Paper streamers
flying from rooftops, paper kites, a slice
of water-melon – this is Tanabata,
festival of stars, the city hung with dreams
and, looking on, the broken mountain.

Yesterday at last we climbed the cop,
stood on the close-cropped turf and saw the world
spread out below – the salt plains and their towns,
a single mill, the rivers to the west
shrouded, and to the east the moors, empty
and shadow-chased. I touched your hip, as though
by chance: imagining a festival,
our stars, our dreams, our city flourishing.

Skizzen / Sketches

I meet her in the courtyard. I have come to Copenhagen to look for the painter, but instead I find her. Cast in bronze, greened by time, standing on her plinth. Half-covered by clematis, standing against the wall in the courtyard of the apartment house, 30 Strandgade, the setting for so many of his best-known paintings, those drifting half-lit interiors. The statue of a young woman, naked, her upper body disappearing, her face almost completely hidden in the tangled creeper. Who is she, how has she come here? On the plinth is inscribed the name of – presumably – the sculptor, but I can't read it. Also the date, 1896. Was that the year the painter, too, came to live here, with his young wife, soon after they married? (Looking this up later, I find that they moved here in 1898, having married in 1891.)

Who is she? Her left arm is down by her side; her right arm is held straight up by her head, her hand hidden somewhere up in the leaves. She's holding a bird, something like a pigeon – a dove maybe? Perhaps she represents Peace? Her face too is hard to make out, hidden by the leaves and the tangle of thin twisting stems that double back, tie themselves to themselves in knots, and camouflaged further by the strange pale streaks of verdigris. I wonder why someone – one of the residents of the apartments – doesn't cut back the creeper, so that she can see out more easily. But then, perhaps she prefers it this way, her face half-concealed, only visible to those who come to enquire, who want to talk to her, to find out who she is. Because there is something a little awful, after all, about the way she is forced to stand there and go on standing, unable to move or to cover herself, the verdigris streaking her thighs, her belly, like the public aftermath of some secret encounter.

I had been trying for a while to find a way to write about the paintings of Vilhelm Hammershøi, to try to express in words what fascinated me about them, particularly his images of the apartment in Strandgade. Those eerily empty, bleached-out rooms with their windows giving onto nothing but a pale blankness, their sequences of doors leading only to more doors, to more rooms – interiors with no exteriors, doors and windows yet no way out. And always, or almost always, the figure of Ida, the painter's wife – yet not Ida, not really, just the figure of a woman, a blocky shape, standing or sitting, and almost always with her back to us, her dark hair pinned up at the back... a figure, a solid body, taking up space inside the space of the room, sometimes apparently engaged in some everyday activity – sitting at a table, sweeping the floor – but always, we feel, not really doing that or doing anything; a presence that is also always an absence, a figure, a woman, yet not really a person. After trying various approaches I finally hit on what then at once seemed the obvious strategy – to try to write from Ida's point of view, from the point of view of this woman who appears in so many of the paintings yet who never really appears as herself, who seems both solidly present and somehow absent, abstracted from herself. Unsure of how or whether the poem was working, I sent a draft to a poet friend, S, who responded with a wonderfully thoughtful, and thought-provoking, reading. Seeing the poem as, among other things, interrogating the act of representation, the relationship between painter and painted, subject and object, she asked what felt like important questions, beginning with precisely this sense of vanishing, of erosion of specificity:

> ... individual psychology or even character is eroded in his paintings: the figures seem to be entirely part of the scene (like a radical extension of Cézanne, who at least allowed them their own colours). I don't know how you feel about this aspect of the painting. Do you feel it is gendered? Would he / did he paint men in this way?

(The answer to this last question seems to be 'almost never' – male figures do appear occasionally in Hammershøi's paintings, but it is the repeated figure of the woman, reduced to a columnar shape – dark hair, bodice, long black skirt – that echoes throughout his work. And this does seem almost inevitable. It is women we associate with domestic interiors – women, not men, who would have spent their days in the enclosed apartments Hammershøi is painting. More, it is women we associate with this half-presence, this turning-away that suggests something eternally elusive – a structure of subject/object relations for which Eurydice is perhaps the ultimate template. In Rilke's poem 'Orpheus. Eurydice. Hermes', Eurydice is always already disappearing, she is becoming earth, coming fully into her own death. There is certainly a possible reading of this poem as a proto-feminist statement – Eurydice, in Rilke's version, no longer recognises Orpheus, much less belongs to him:

She was no longer that woman with blue eyes
who once had echoed through the poet's songs,
no longer the wide couch's scent and island,
and that man's property no longer.

The poem enacts a paradox: Eurydice belongs not to Orpheus but to
herself, and yet it is really the earth – that is, death – to which she
belongs:

She was already loosened like long hair,
poured out like fallen rain,
shared like a limitless supply.

She was already root.

The poem ends with Eurydice seen again from Orpheus's perspective,
a small, lost figure, 'already walking back along the path'. It seems
very difficult, even as a thought-experiment, to reverse this structure
– to imagine a female subject who pursues, or constructs, a fleeting,
elusive, male object.)

Noting how much she enjoyed the aesthetic harmony of the
paintings, S went on to press further questions – addressing herself,
I think, as much as me.

Does that aestheticisation erode the subject? I can't find it in
me spiritually to condemn this approach to the subject, because
all art involves controlling a reality for an aesthetic. To what
degree must that aesthetic be governed by morality? And within
that question I suppose another: governed by our morality now?

'I have no answers to any of those questions', she wrote. And nor do
I. I continue to find the paintings compelling, and the mystery, the
elusiveness, of the turned-away figure of the woman is certainly part
of this. Perhaps, indeed, it could be read as a kind of resistance to
representation, to interpretation – as a kind of self-possession. Yet
the poem in the end formed itself around the sense of an ongoing
loss of self (S's use of the word *erosion* seemed perfect here). In the
Strandgade courtyard, meanwhile, I feel both moved and unsettled
by my encounter with the bronze figure of the woman – not eroded

but stained, streaked, mottled, in a particularly disturbing way; and, crucially, not turned away – unable to turn away. She is beautiful, yes, but she is also deeply, painfully exposed.

*

A half-hour train journey north of Copenhagen, to the museum of modern art: Louisiana (the name apparently in tribute to the three wives of the original owner of the house, one Alexander Brun – all three, implausibly enough, being named Louise). The white house, extended into the long glass galleries, the whole thing landscaped around the sculpture park and looking out across the Øresund. Sweden a faint line, a glimpse of a white city. In the south gallery, a series of rooms like dark boxes with magical boxes inside them. Time runs both backwards and forwards, everything pivoting around one point, 1969. Fifty years since people first walked on the moon. (And significant for me in another way – fifty years since I was born.) Here are maps, charts, drawings, imaginings. Daguerrotypes inside velvet-lined cases. Here are the gorgeous darkblue mysteries of Joseph Cornell's boxes, with the flickering 1902 psychedelia of Georges Méliès' *Le Voyage dans la lune* playing out in reflection on the glass. And here the beautiful optical illusion of Max Ernst's *Naissance d'une galaxie*, the bluewhite disc of the moon pixelated and strobing, the shadows like pieces of fallen night sky, and the date on the painting, 1969 – a shock, I hadn't thought of Ernst still living when I was born, I had thought of him as already an old man, white-haired, when he first met Leonora Carrington in 1937 – but I realise that he was younger then than I am now.

In the next room, the moon flickers over the white wall, jittery, seems to hang in the trees as though caught on wire, burning at the edges, now red, now blue – Malena Szlam's *Lunar Almanac*. Another wall is printed with omens, warnings, prohibitions:

> *You mustn't see the moon through a window. When my father had seen the moon through the window, the farm caught fire.*

> *If your bed stands such that the full moon can shine on it, you must cover the windows before going to bed, for if the full moon shines on the face of a sleeper it can twist his neck.*

A pregnant woman must not sit and piss and look up at the moon.

And throughout the gallery, the strangely haunting piano music. The grand piano at the entrance to the room, seemingly playing by itself. The score on the wall, translated to the dots and dashes of Morse code. The left-hand sheet full; the right-hand sheet fractured, with gaps, blanks in the code. Katie Paterson's *Earth-Moon-Earth (Moonlight Sonata Reflected from the Surface of the Moon)*: Beethoven's music encoded, beamed up to the moon, and sent back again, but raggedly, parts of the sonic information lost in the craters and shadows of the moon's damaged surface.

I think of A's mother. July 1969. A young woman in a terraced house in Liverpool, pregnant with her third child, waiting in the particular aloneness that is waiting to go into labour. Sitting on the sofa in the early hours, the two children half-asleep, brought downstairs to watch the images unfolding, to listen to the broken, fuzzy transmission, the words sent back through two hundred thousand miles. And then, over the next months, the sense of travelling further and further into aloneness, the terrible cold distance that is named post-natal depression. The shock treatment to snap her out of it, to bring her back to normality.

(In her autobiographical novel *Faces in the Water*, based on the years she spent incarcerated in mental hospitals, Janet Frame describes in detail the terror this particular treatment held for the patients:

> Every morning I woke in dread, waiting for the day nurse to go on her rounds and announce from the list of names in her hand whether or not I was for shock treatment, the new and fashionable means of quieting people and of making them realise that orders are to be obeyed and floors are to be polished without anyone protesting and faces are made to be fixed into smiles and weeping is a crime. Waiting in the early morning, in the black-capped frosted hours, was like waiting for the pronouncement of a death sentence.)

From New Zealand in the 1940s to Liverpool, England, in 1969. And soon after the shock treatment, to try to cure the loss of self identified as post-natal depression, the first symptoms of another

71

kind of loss – the syndrome identified and described in 1817 by the English surgeon James Parkinson as 'the shaking palsy', but which now carries his name. The nerve cells damaged, the vital messenger, dopamine, not being produced, the transmissions to the motor system no longer getting through. Progressively more locked-in by an extreme form of Parkinson's, probably though not provably caused by the ECT, A's mother was put into a residential home for elderly people, although she wasn't old; when she died, in 1995, of pneumonia, she was still only 56. Here in the gallery at Louisiana, the *Moonlight Sonata* plays raggedly on.

★

From Copenhagen, south by train towards Hamburg. A journey through flatlands and across water. The line follows the eastern coast of Zealand, then crosses the strait to Falster, then crosses another strait to Lolland – 'low land', an island whose highest point is just eighty feet above sea level. At Rødby, on the southern coast of Lolland, the conductor politely announces – in Danish, German, and English – that there will be a short wait; then, with a minimum of fuss, the train is driven onto the ferry, drawing into its allotted narrow space between the lorries on deck 3. We leave our baggage on the train, which is locked for the duration of the 45-minute crossing to Germany, and head up on deck.

The Fehmarn Belt is calm; Scandlines ferries placidly make their way to and fro between Rødby and Puttgarden. Our ferry is named, aptly enough, the *Schleswig-Holstein*. In the Statens Museum for Kunst, in Copenhagen, I had read that the threatened breakaway by the duchies of Schleswig and Holstein, their desire for stronger connections with the powerful Prussian state, was among the factors contributing to the national crisis faced by Denmark in the early nineteenth century, a crisis that led, paradoxically, to the patriotic flourishing of art and culture that subsequently came to be known as the Danish Golden Age. The Schleswig-Holstein question, the historical back-and-forth of these disputed borderlands, would continue to play out for another century and more. From Puttgarden the train rolls quietly on southwards through the former duchy of Holstein, now part of the German *Land* of Schleswig-Holstein, the

72

flat fields of rapeseed identical to those of Zealand, of Lolland. Half an hour south of Lübeck, and exactly on time at quarter past four, the train arrives at its final destination, the city-state of Hamburg.

★

Next day, at the Kunsthalle, I speak to the man at the counter in German, but he replies in English. I mock-grimace, tell him that I really need to work harder on my German pronunciation. I say it jokingly but it matters. I don't want to be immediately identifiable as British, I don't want the immediate polite response of switching into English. More than anything I don't want to be trapped in one language-world. I want to be able to exist in another language, however imperfectly; to know, in however limited a way, the different world that another language opens up.

★

In the basement gallery: Lili Fischer. *Alles beginnt mit Zeichnen.* Everything begins with drawing. Large sheets of paper, torn perhaps from sketchbooks, and on them, everything becoming something else. In Fischer's work everything is about the line, the way it moves – the sense of the hand in motion, the eye, thought itself. Sketches on music-paper, text scrawled over old account books. Sketches of plants, of trees whipped by the wind; of cloud-formations, of rocks and earth. And human figures – moving, dancing, over the gallery walls. Fischer is also a dancer, a choreographer. Her project books, displayed in the gallery, show her dancing with a witch's broom – a kind of hex-dance, a spell created by motion, by the body sketching itself in space. A spell brings about a change, a transformation, and everything here is about transformation, everything is provisional and becoming something else. These lines, drawn, written, danced, with so much energy – a kind of half-language, a language in which nothing stays still. And the question for me, as always: how to bring this movement, this constant transformation, into writing? into poetry?

★

Upstairs, in the modern art galleries, something of a shock to encounter again the extraordinary 1930 self-portrait by Anita Rée. I had seen it here a year ago, as part of the first ever retrospective dedicated to Rée, but hadn't expected to see it again, forgetting that the Kunsthalle owns some of her works.

Born in Hamburg in 1885, Rée was the daughter of a Venezuelan (presumably Catholic) mother and a Jewish father. Both Anita and her older sister Emilie were baptised as Protestants, but by 1931 that wouldn't stop the Nazi-leaning newspaper the *Hamburger Tageblatt* from objecting to a triptych designed by Rée being installed in a church in the Hamburg suburb of Langenhorn. In 1932, depressed and isolated, feeling herself increasingly under threat as the Nazis tightened their grip, Rée went to live on the island of Sylt, in North Frisia, where she drew and painted bleak, bleached-out watercolours of the dunes, the grey sea and heavy sky, and where on 12 December 1933 she committed suicide. I know that she killed herself, in practical fact, by taking an overdose of Veronal. In my mind, though, she became part of the island, its bleak dunes, its grey sea, grey sky. She abstracted herself, eroded herself, erased herself, walked further and further into the island until she didn't come out.

I had never heard of Anita Rée before stumbling on the exhibition, but was fascinated by her work, especially her strikingly expressive portraits, which shared something of the power and challenge of Frida Kahlo's images of herself, but were painted in a very different idiom, a combination of modernist stylisation with Renaissance icons – faces as strong oval shapes, planes of rich flat colour, bronze powder adding metallic sheen. Especially in the oil paintings she made in Positano, in southern Italy, during the 1920s, Rée seemed to be celebrating colour and sensuality; but also, with her precise attention to outline, her building-up of rich colour through layers of careful application of pigment and glazes, clearly situating herself within the classical European tradition of Renaissance religious art. By contrast, the landscapes she painted in her last years on Sylt are scrubby watercolours, done with a dry brush and no underdrawing – rough patches of colour, a palette shrunk to greys and greens and dull ochre yellows. The landscape is empty, the scenes devoid of human life – only a few scattered sheep, the sketches seem to say, can survive here.

It was also in her last years on Sylt that Rée completed a series of self-portraits in pencil, images that had arrested me as soon as I walked into the exhibition. Just sketches, lines on paper, these were so different from her earlier self-portraits in oils, and yet extraordinarily expressive – her face reduced to its essentials, the heavy brows, the hooded eyes, and the peculiar sidelong up-and-under gaze, that seemed to pose a question, even a challenge, to the viewer. The portraits seemed poised between presence and absence – sketchy, incomplete, a self in the process of disappearing, and yet with such a definite sense of challenge. Rée in these drawings looks world-weary, resigned to the impossibility of continuing, and yet there is also something absolutely defiant in those sidelong glances, that cocked head. *Well*, she seems to be asking, *Can you say I was wrong?*

I had bought the catalogue, read the essays, studied the images. I had tried to write a poem about Rée on Sylt. I was fascinated by the strange, shifting nature of Sylt itself – originally part of the intertidal zone, constantly shifting between land and sea, it became an island following the *Grote Mandrenke*, the Great Flood (literally, 'great drowning of men'), of January 1362, when a massive storm-surge flooded the east coast of England and the west coast of Jutland, drowning towns and creating islands. Ever since then Sylt has been eroding, giving itself gradually back to the sea; now a popular tourist destination, it is subject to constant attempts to prevent further erosion, attempts to shore it up, preserve its solidity. I saw the parallels between Rée and the island itself, but I couldn't seem to make them work out in the poem. I couldn't figure out what I wanted to say about those pencil portraits, those scrubby watercolours, ultimately about Rée's suicide on the island, her decision to disappear.

Now, a year after first encountering those images, I encounter again the 1930 self-portrait – perhaps the last image Rée painted of herself in oils? – and am struck all over again by the paradox it seems to present. In this head-and-shoulders portrait Rée depicts herself naked – unusually for her, facing the viewer straight on. Her left arm is crossed over her body, hiding her breasts; her right hand rests on her chin, her face propped in her hand. She gazes at us directly out of her large, dark, deep-set eyes, under the Kahlo-heavy brows. Her expression is impossible to read. The image is stark, vulnerable, but also powerful in its strong shapes, its sense – again – of challenge. The background is yellowish-green – somehow a menacing, a clinical, colour. The verticals (folds in a curtain, perhaps) are off-vertical, slanting in towards her. It's as though she is descending some strange confined space. She is a woman trapped inside a narrowing future – she knows it, and, gazing out, she makes us know it. But the most striking detail of all, perhaps, is the earring she wears: this dark-pink coral earring, when she is otherwise naked, its colour an absolute contrast to the greenish-yellow background – surely a small but definite gesture of defiance.

★

Friday night. T and I, in a bar on the twentieth floor of a shiny new hotel building, near the waterfront. The glass and chrome building is, as he says, a bit chi-chi, but the views from the bar are spectacular. Also the music is good – insistent enough to give everything a pulse, not so loud that we can't talk easily. The conversation slides between German and English, a mix that gets looser as the evening goes on. We are drinking a rum concoction called a St-Pauli-Killer; the cocktails come in tall glasses, with glass straws, the first time I've encountered this. We are standing by the floor-to-ceiling glass windows looking down at the city. Early November, the night is *nebelig*, misty; everything a little blurred at the edges. To our left, the gaudy neon of the Reeperbahn; beyond it, the huge fairground at the Hamburger Dom, the Ferris wheel, the tower ride that looks terrifyingly high, the lights whirling and flashing demoniacally. Directly below us is a new development of low-rise housing; lights are on in the apartments and I wonder whether any of the people there are looking up, watching us. To our right is the dock road, the landing-stages; lights along the waterfront, lights of the pleasure boats; stretching away into the distance, the lights of the shipyards; and the ghost-echo of all of it in the wide black gleam of the river.

The river Elbe rises in the mountains known in Czech as the Krkonoše, in Polish as the Karkonosze, in German as the Riesengebirge. It flows south and then west through what is now the Czech Republic, then north-west through Germany, via Dresden, Meissen, Wittenberg, Dessau, Magdeburg, to Hamburg, finally emptying into the North Sea at Cuxhaven. The main ridge of the Riesengebirge mountain chain forms the border between present-day Poland and the Czech Republic; historically, the border between Silesia, to the north, and Bohemia, to the south – the way taken by the Elbe. Connecting Bohemia to the North Sea, the Elbe in a sense makes truth of Ingeborg Bachmann's visionary topography in her late poem 'Böhmen liegt am Meer' – 'Bohemia Lies by the Sea'.

Bachmann was born in 1926 in Klagenfurt, in Austria. Her father had been a member of the NSDAP; she would later state that the experience of seeing the Nazis march into the city square in 1938 marked the end of her childhood. Her friend, reader, writer, lover (theirs was a relationship conducted more through the exchange of writing than through actual physical proximity) would be Paul Celan – Celan, born in Czernowitz in 1920, his parents killed in Nazi camps, a German speaker who would turn the German language inside out in an attempt to articulate the impossible, and who, finally unable to continue 'surviving' the Holocaust, would commit suicide by drowning in the Seine in 1970. Bachmann's first collection of poems was published to great acclaim in 1953, when she was only 27, followed by a second collection in 1956, but she then turned to prose, becoming known as a writer of novels, essays and short stories; though she continued to write poems, she didn't publish them.

'Bohemia Lies by the Sea', though, one of the last poems Bachmann completed, could only have been written as a poem; its form is an essential part of what it is, what it does. It takes its starting point from Shakespeare's (erroneous – or fantastical) description of Bohemia, in *The Winter's Tale*, as 'a desert country near the sea', and plays on the idea to construct a vision of hope, a refusal of limits, of borders, ultimately a refusal of pernicious ideas of purity. The poem enacts a kind of dance in which the key words, the key ideas, keep circling and returning and transforming into their opposites, and in which self, world and word are not separate or separable:

If it's not me, it's another who is just as good as me.

If a word borders on me here, I'll let it border.
If Bohemia still lies by the sea, I'll believe in the sea again.
And, still believing in the sea, I can hope for land.

If it's me, then it's anyone and might as well be me.
I want nothing more for myself. I want to go under.

Under – that means the sea, where I will find Bohemia again.
Finally grounded, I wake up in peace.
From deep inside, I know I'm unabandoned.

For me, Bachmann's poem has exactly the transformative energies of Lili Fischer's drawings, of her dances – it is one thing becoming another, refusing to stay still, refusing to accept the limits put upon it. The poem calls on, celebrates, the ones who won't be tied down – 'Come, you Bohemians, sailors and dock whores and unmoored ships'. It ends with a hopeful vision of belonging as not-belonging, the poet under water yet 'finally grounded', 'held by nothing' yet 'unabandoned':

I still border on a word and on another land;
I border, like little else, on everything more and more,

a Bohemian, a vagabond who has and is held by nothing,
whose only gift was to find, from a dubious sea, my chosen
     land.

Back in the bar on the twentieth floor, I look out over the Elbe. Tomorrow I must fly back home, back to the island country (or rather an unequal, uneasy union of countries) currently tearing itself apart over questions of identity, of borders and belonging, fantasies of a sovereignty that never existed and never could, people set against each other in a struggle it's hard to see a way out of. Tomorrow I must fly back. For tonight, though, I am here – or at least someone is here, holding a tall glass with a glass straw, her reflection blurred in the black glass of the night sky, looking out over the lights of the city, the river's black gleam. If she can belong anywhere, she can belong here; and if she can be anyone, she might as well be me.

November 2018

Notes

'Painting the Sitting-Room Door'
Thanks to Eleanor Rees for the inspiration for this poem.

'Hors-la-loi'
Based on a photograph by Lee Miller of Leonora Carrington and Max Ernst at Lambe Creek, Cornwall, 1937.

'Being Mary Lennox'
Mary Lennox is the protagonist in Frances Hodgson Burnett's *The Secret Garden* (1911).

'Rhododendron Garden'
The italicised text is from the National Trust signage at Plas Newydd, Anglesey.

'Blueprint'
Some phrases in this piece are taken or adapted from published novels.

'Hotel Apostrophe'
Inspired by a real building, in Montolieu, Aude, France. Thanks to Sarah Hymas for introducing me to it.

'Chinese White'
The pigment Chinese white (zinc oxide) was introduced by the Winsor & Newton company in 1834 and was hugely successful. The testimonial quoted here is from the painter J.D. Harding (see http://www.winsornewton.com/uk/discover/articles-and-inspiration/spotlight-on-chinese-white). Henry Newton, the co-founder (with chemist William Winsor) of Winsor & Newton, was the grandfather of the painter Algernon Cecil Newton (see 'Aftermaths').

'Funeral Procession of Mourners and Musicians'
These figurines are on display at the Lady Lever Art Gallery, Port Sunlight, Wirral.

'Aftermaths'
After the first section ('They said *a toy London*'), which responds to Newton's work generally, the sections respond to the following paintings: *The Regent's Canal, Paddington* (1930); *Summer Morning* (1942); *Spring Morning, Campden Hill* (1940); *Bourdon House from Berkeley Square, London* (1932); *The Surrey Canal, Camberwell* (1935); *A Gap in the Hedge* (1960).

'Letter to Anna'
Partly inspired by Vilhelm Hammershøi's 1885 painting *Portrait of a Young Woman. The Artist's Sister, Anna Hammershøi*, though the situation depicted in the poem has no connection with the historical Anna.

'What Can We Still Do'
Text collaged from Ingeborg Bachmann and Paul Celan, *Correspondence* (trans. Wieland Hoban; New York: Seagull, 2010).

'Skizzen / Sketches'
I am very grateful to Sasha Dugdale for her insightful comments on Hammershøi and the wider issues around representation in art, and for allowing me to quote from them in this piece. I am also grateful to Peter Davidson for encouraging me to think, and write, about some of the topics here.

The translation of Rilke's 'Orpheus. Eurydice. Hermes' is by Stephen Mitchell.

The moon exhibition: *Månen/The Moon*, at Louisiana Museum of Modern Art, Humlebaek, 13 September 2018–20 January 2019.

Lili Fischer, *Alles beginnt mit Zeichnen*, Hamburger Kunsthalle, 19 October 2018–10 February 2019.

Anita Rée, *Retrospektive*, Hamburger Kunsthalle, 6 October 2017–4 February 2018. Catalogue edited by Karin Schick (Hamburger Kunsthalle/Prestel Verlag, 2017).

Translation of Ingeborg Bachmann's 'Böhmen liegt am Meer' by Frank Beck, published in *PN Review* 228 (2016). My discussion of Bachmann draws on Peter Filkins' introduction to *Darkness Spoken: Ingeborg Bachmann, The Collected Poems* (trans. and ed. Peter Filkins; Zephyr Press, 2006).

With love, and thanks, to the Schulze family in Hamburg.

Acknowledgements

Some of these poems, or versions of them, have previously appeared in the following publications: *Blackbox Manifold*; *Eborakon*; *Magma*; *The Manchester Review*; *Shearsman*; *The Caught Habits of Language: An Entertainment for W.S. Graham for him having reached One Hundred* (Donut Press, 2018); *The Forward Book of Poetry 2019* (Forward Arts Foundation, 2018); *The Valley Press Anthology of Prose Poetry* (Valley Press, 2019). Some of the poems were published in my pamphlet *In the Glasshouse* (HappenStance, 2016) and in the booklet accompanying the CD *If You Put Out Your Hand* (with Sharron Kraus; Wounded Wolf Press, 2016).

I am very grateful to all the people who have generously read and discussed these poems with me: Tara Bergin, Lucy Burnett, Sasha Dugdale, Ian Duhig, Caroline Hawkridge, Martin Heslop, Seán Hewitt, Sarah Hymas, Grevel Lindop, Andrew McMillan, Helena Nelson, Ruby Robinson, Pauline Rowe, and especially Judith Willson.